What-If Science?

Cynthia O'Brien

Lerner Publications ◆ Minneapolis

Lerner Publications Company
An imprint of Lerner Publishing Group, Inc.
241 First Avenue North
Minneapolis, MN 55401 USA

For reading levels and more information, look up this title at www.lernerbooks.com.

Main body text set in Adrianna Regular.
Typeface provided by Chank.

Library of Congress Cataloging-in-Publication Data

Names: O'Brien, Cynthia (Cynthia J.) author
Title: Could humans live forever? / Cynthia O'Brien.
Description: Minneapolis : Lerner Publications, [2026] | Series: Searchlight books. What-if science? | Includes bibliographical references and index. | Audience: Ages 8–11 | Audience: Grades 4–6 | Summary: "What would it take for humans to live forever? Discover two ways we could become immortal-programming our brains into computers or improving medical technology-and the challenges of making these happen"—Provided by publisher.
Identifiers: LCCN 2025011294 (print) | LCCN 2025011295 (ebook) | ISBN 9798765688977 lib. bdg. | ISBN 9798348029173 pbk | ISBN 9798765698105 epub
Subjects: LCSH: Death—Juvenile literature | Aging—Prevention—Juvenile literature | Immortality—Juvenile literature
Classification: LCC QP87 .O27 2026 (print) | LCC QP87 (ebook) | DDC 306.9—dc23/eng/20250716

LC record available at https://lccn.loc.gov/2025011294
LC ebook record available at https://lccn.loc.gov/2025011295

Manufactured in the United States of America
1 - CG - 12/15/25

Table of Contents

Chapter 1

A LONG LIFE

It is many years in the future. Robots are everywhere, working alongside teachers, nurses, and other professionals. But these aren't regular robots—these robots are people who have replaced their human bodies with robot parts. Their computer brains are exact copies of their human brains. In this way, they can live forever.

At the moment this is impossible. But it raises an important question: Is a human brain in a robot body still a person? The human brain is made up of billions of nerve cells called neurons. Neurons send and receive messages from all over the body. This allows the brain to control everything we do. The brain holds memories, too. In many ways, it makes us who we are. The technology to make computer copies of our brains doesn't exist yet. We need to keep our brains and bodies healthy to live longer lives.

Regular exercise keeps the body strong and healthy.

Sunscreen protects the skin from being harmed by the sun.

Why Do Humans Age?

Aging involves the trillions of cells that make up the human body. Cells die, change, or become damaged over time. They stop working as they should. Aging happens for many reasons. Human bodies wear down with use. Lack of exercise or eating unhealthy food can also cause a person to age faster. The environment is important, too. The sun damages unprotected skin.

The Oldest People

Around the world, most people are expected to live almost seventy-three years. Many people live much longer than this. A woman in France lived until she was 122, and there may be other people who have lived longer. Scientists believe that half of all five-year-olds alive in 2025 will live to be one hundred.

JEANNE CALMENT WAS THE WORLD'S OLDEST PERSON WHEN SHE DIED AGED 122.

Lessons from Nature

Some animals live for a long time. The glass sponge can live more than eleven thousand years. Greenland sharks can be more than four hundred years old. Scientists study animals like these to find out how they live such long lives. They look for clues that could help humans live much longer.

Other animals can cure diseases with their own bodies! Elephants rarely get cancer. Their bodies repair cells in ways that human bodies cannot. Scientists are studying elephants to find out how humans could fight cancer.

Greenland sharks can be 24 feet (7.3 m) long.

Deep Dive

Decoding the Brain

Linking the brain to artificial intelligence (AI) systems can help to make people's lives better. Due to an illness, Casey Harrell had lost the ability to speak clearly. In 2023, scientists helped Harrell to speak again. They implanted devices called electrodes in Harrell's brain to connect his brain signals to a computer. When his brain sent a signal to speak, the computer picked up the brainwaves and produced words. The computer learned Harrell's natural voice from old recordings.

Special technology allowed Casey Harrell to speak again.

Chapter 2

MEDICINES AND TECHNOLOGY

Long ago, many people did not live to older ages. Medicines, sanitation, and medical tools have changed this. Doctors and other scientists also know much more about the human body than ever before. They are developing new technologies and treatments to help people live longer. Some scientists believe that future medicines and technology could help humans live one thousand years or even longer.

Medicine

Medicines have saved lives for thousands of years. Ancient people used plants to treat the sick. Even today, about 40 percent of medicines come from or include plants. Penicillin is a life-saving antibiotic. It comes from mold, a type of fungus. Many other medicines are combinations of chemicals. It can take many years to develop and test new medicines. They must work and be safe to use before doctors give them to patients.

This mold makes the antibiotic penicillin.

Stopping Disease

One important invention that extended human life was the vaccine. Vaccines teach the body's immune system to remember and fight diseases. In 1796, Edward Jenner created a vaccine against smallpox, a deadly disease. This was the first successful vaccine. Others followed, including vaccines for measles and diphtheria. In the past fifty years, vaccines have saved about 154 million lives around the world.

Edward Jenner was an English doctor and scientist.

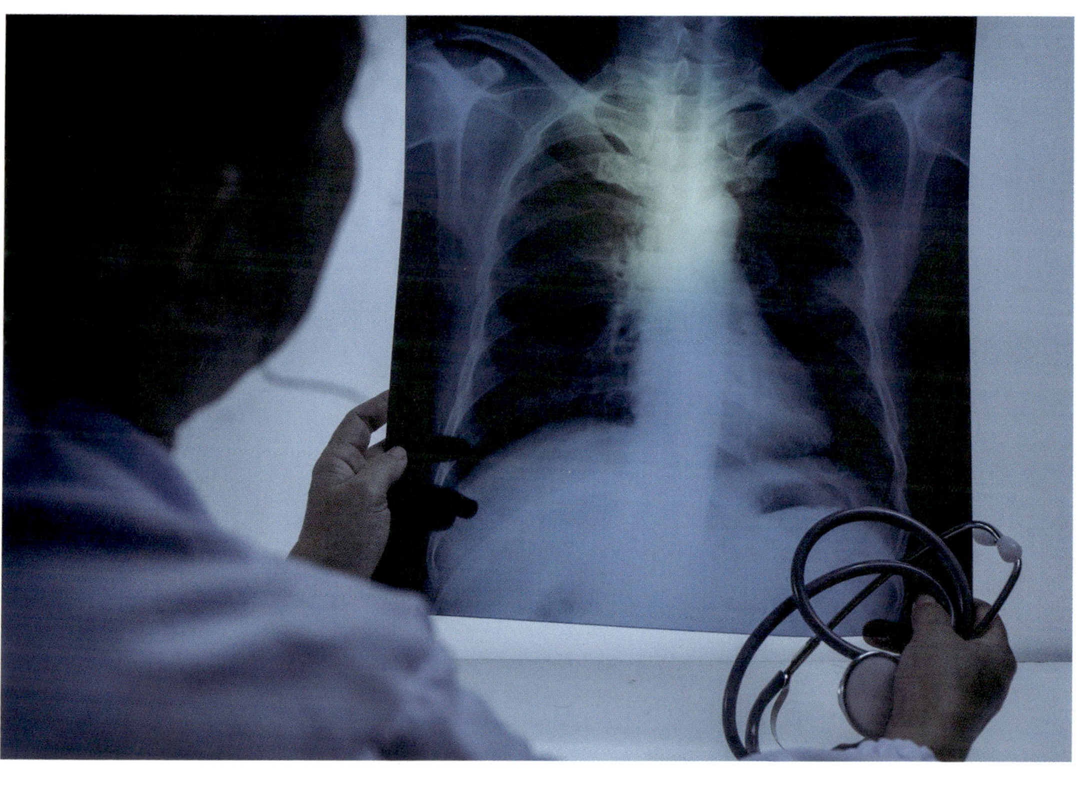

X-RAYS SHOW BONES AND ORGANS INSIDE THE BODY.

Finding the Problem

There are many tests to find out what is going on inside the body. Imaging tests take pictures of the inside of the human body. X-rays were invented in 1895, and other imaging technology followed.

Ultrasounds, CT scans, and MRIs are other imaging tests. An MRI produces a picture of organs, tissues, bones, and blood vessels. It can show diseases and injuries so that doctors know how to treat them.

AN MRI SCANNER USES A MAGNET AND RADIO WAVES TO MAKE IMAGES.

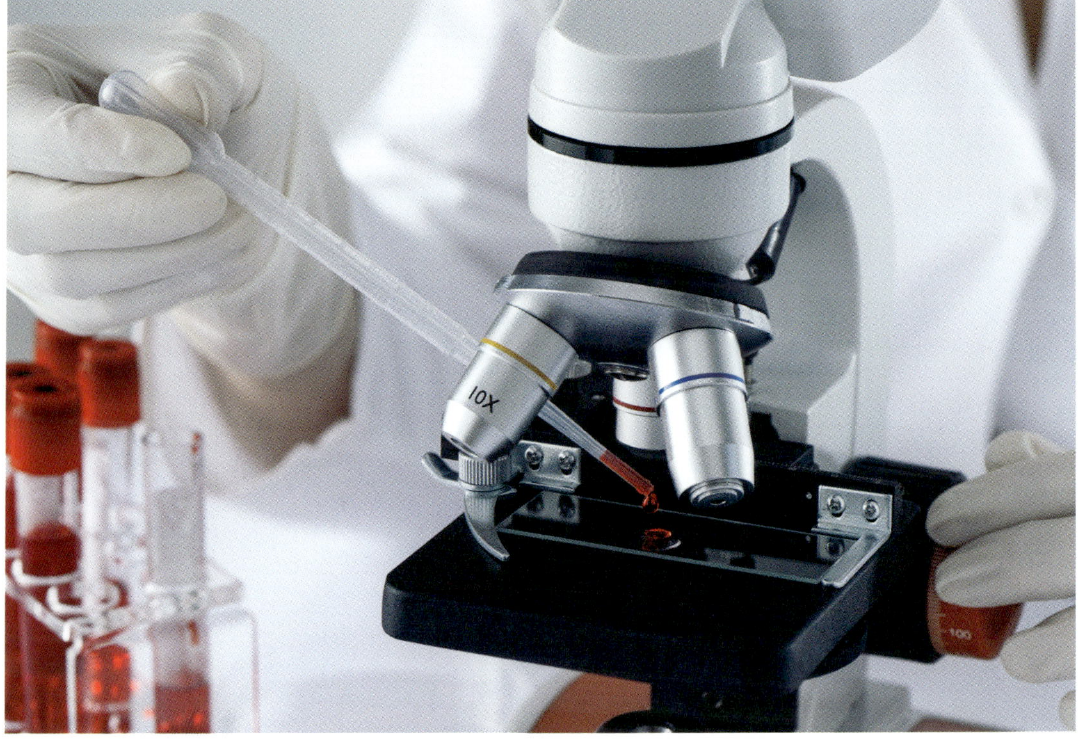

BLOOD TESTS CAN HELP TO CHECK THAT MEDICINE IS WORKING.

Blood tests tell doctors a lot about a person's health. They can detect diseases or reveal that an organ, such as the liver, is not working as it should. Scientists examine blood in a laboratory. If doctors find a problem, there may be medicines or operations that can help.

Under the Knife

Hundreds of years ago, many people did not survive operations. There was no anesthesia. This is a drug that puts patients to sleep during an operation and stops them from feeling pain. Surgeries were also dangerous because people didn't keep operation rooms or equipment clean. Germs could enter a patient's wound and spread through the body. Today, surgery is very common and safe. Doctors can repair the body, remove harmful diseases, and replace organs. This has helped millions of people to live longer, healthier lives.

Surgeons wear special clothes to stop the spread of germs.

Deep Dive

Computer Doctors

Some doctors use AI to help them diagnose diseases early. AI systems can spot problems that are not easy for people to see. This is especially important for diseases like cancer. If cancer is found early, people are more likely to survive. AI systems also save time by learning and analyzing a huge amount of information in seconds.

AI can help doctors diagnose illnesses.

Chapter 3

BIONIC HUMANS

Bionics is an area of science. It makes artificial systems that copy natural ones. In medicine, this can mean implants, prostheses, and other technology. Pacemakers help the heart keep a regular beat. Cochlear implants are electronic devices that help some deaf people to hear.

Retinal implants replace the retina—the part of the eye that senses light and sends signals to the brain. Retinal implants help people with damaged retinas to see again.

COCHLEAR IMPLANTS PICK UP SOUNDS AND SEND SIGNALS TO THE BRAIN.

Brain Power

Diseases, injuries, and accidents are some of the reasons that people lose parts of their bodies. Long ago, people who needed a new limb, such as an arm, wore a prosthetic made of wood, iron, or leather. These parts were very uncomfortable. Modern prostheses are made from materials such as carbon fiber. They are lighter and more flexible. They have electronic parts that move easily.

Lightweight prosthetic limbs let the wearer take part in sports.

AI could allow people with prostheses to feel if something is hot or cold.

AI can create artificial nerves, linking brain signals to prostheses. Brain signals travel through the body's nervous system. The signals reach the muscles the body uses to move. When people lose a limb, a hand, or a foot, the signals have nowhere to go. Using AI, doctors can connect the signals to the prostheses so the brain can control them. Scientists are also developing artificial skin with sensors that will give people a sense of touch.

Tiny Technology

Nanotechnology describes technology made on an extremely small scale. Nanobots are about twenty times smaller than a red blood cell. They can be made of biological and other materials that are safe to use in the human body. Scientists believe that nanobots could have many uses. Nanobots could take medicine into the body. They may also help repair cells and get rid of damaged ones. This could help the body's organs and tissues to stay healthy. Healthy cells could slow down or stop aging.

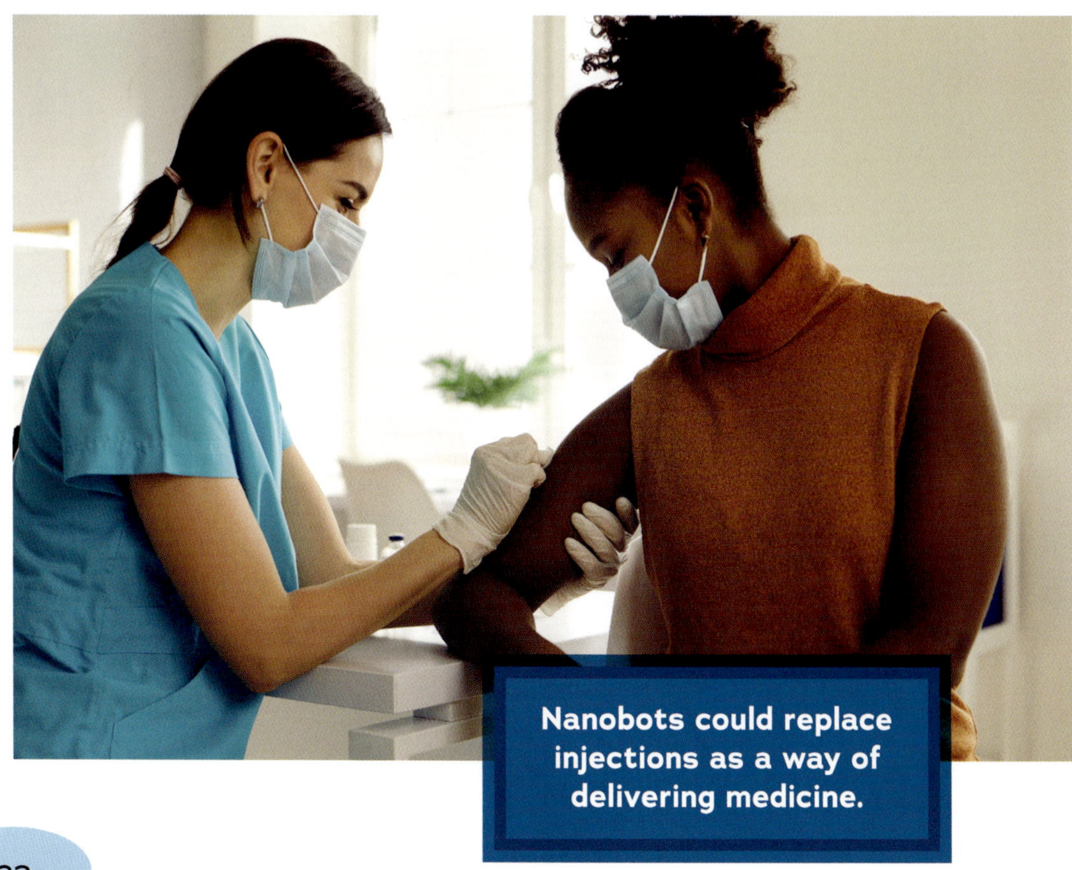

Nanobots could replace injections as a way of delivering medicine.

Chapter 4

LIVING FOREVER

The immortal jellyfish is a tiny creature that lives in warm waters around the world. This jellyfish has the amazing ability to become young again. It drops to the ocean floor and becomes a polyp, a baby jellyfish. Its cells change and enable it to grow into an adult. This jellyfish can do this over and over again.

Changing Cells

People cannot decide to change their cells and become babies again. Instead, scientists are working on different ways to repair or change cells that cause aging. Most human cells divide about forty to sixty times. After this, the cells are too old to work properly, and the cells die. Cells contain genes. With gene therapy, scientists can take out damaged parts of the gene and reprogram it. Or they can use genes to remove diseased cells. This helps to stop, treat, or cure diseases.

Scientists study the immortal jellyfish to find out how it becomes young again.

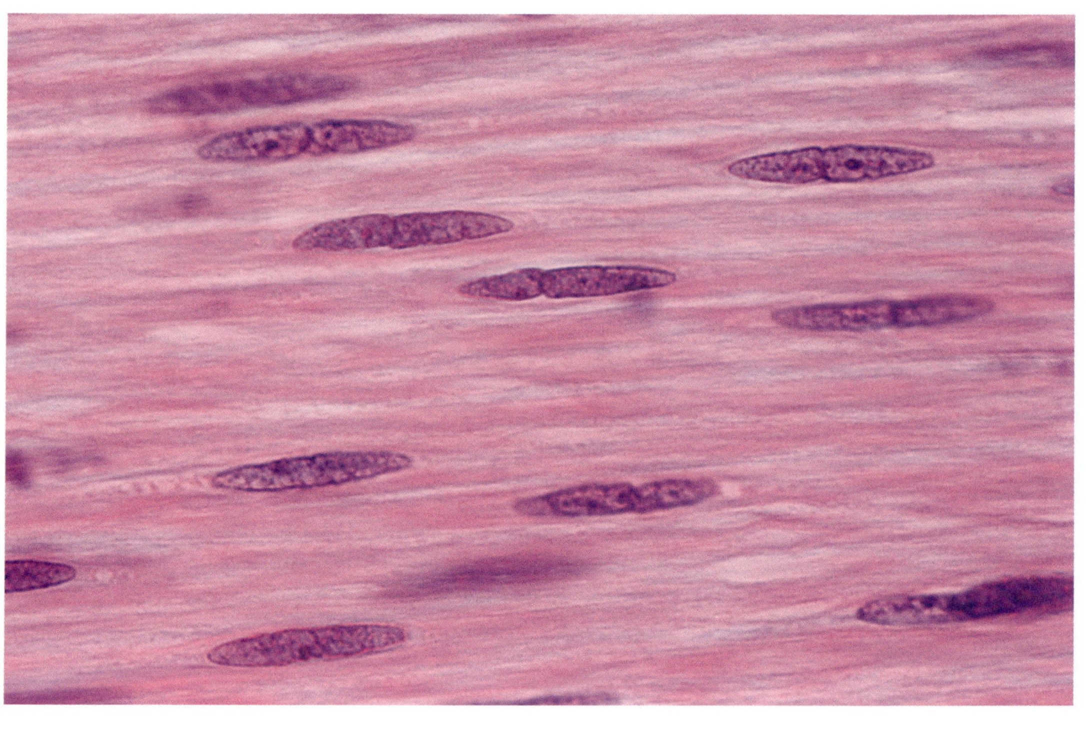

STEM CELLS CAN BE USED TO GROW MUSCLE CELLS LIKE THESE.

Stem cells are another focus. Stem cells can make copies of themselves many times. They can also make more than two hundred different types of cells, such as blood and muscle cells. Stem cells repair tissues and keep organs healthy. Scientists can grow stem cells and use them to treat blood diseases such as leukemia.

Spotlight On:
Altos Labs

Altos Labs launched in 2022 with a team of leading scientists. One of the scientists is Juan Carlos Izpisúa Belmonte. Belmonte believes that, eventually, Altos may help people to stop aging. Meanwhile, the company is focused on keeping people healthy. They are reprogramming cells to make them healthy again. This could help treat diseases, and maybe prevent them from happening.

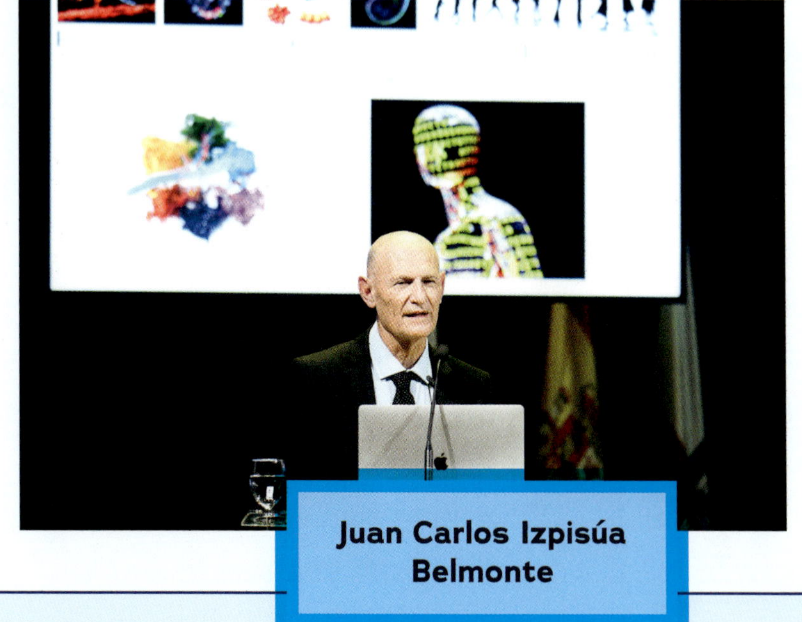

Juan Carlos Izpisúa Belmonte

Making Organs

Surgeons performed the first successful organ transplant in 1954. They transplanted a kidney into a patient whose own kidneys were failing. Heart, lung, and pancreas transplants followed. By 2022, doctors in the United States had performed one million transplants. These transplants were biological, meaning the organs came from another person. Artificial organs are made of plastics or metals, or they can be built using living materials such as cells. Scientists are working on making artificial organs, such as hearts and livers, using 3D printers.

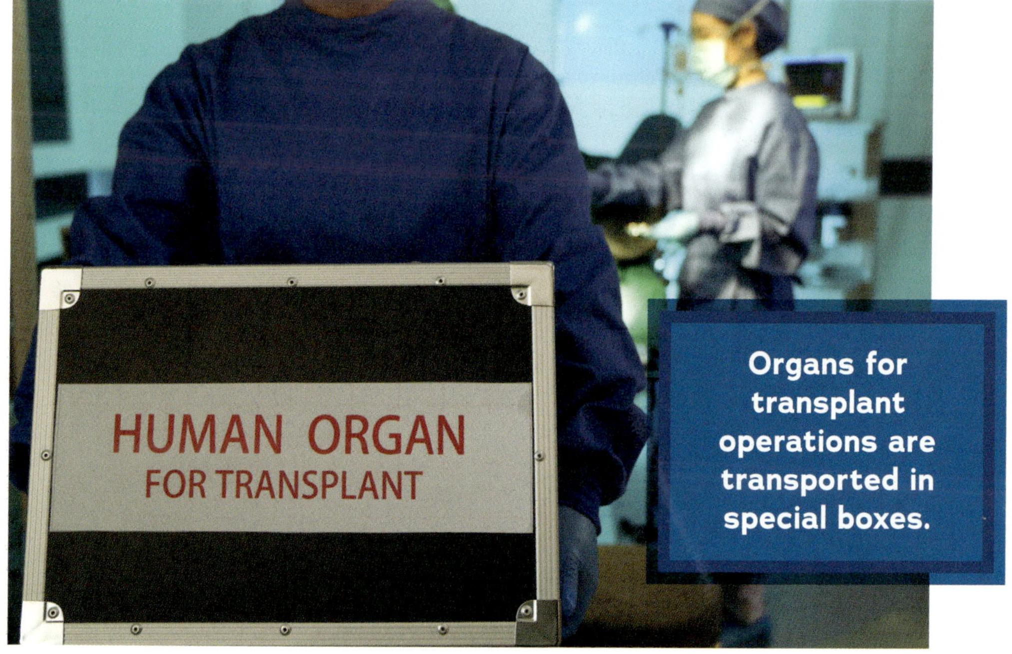

Organs for transplant operations are transported in special boxes.

Frozen in Time

Some people have their bodies frozen after they die. They hope they can be brought back to life in the future. This is called cryonics. Others believe in freezing the brain so scientists can upload it to a computer in the future. So far, both these options are impossible. Meanwhile, science is working toward creating longer, healthier lives for everyone.

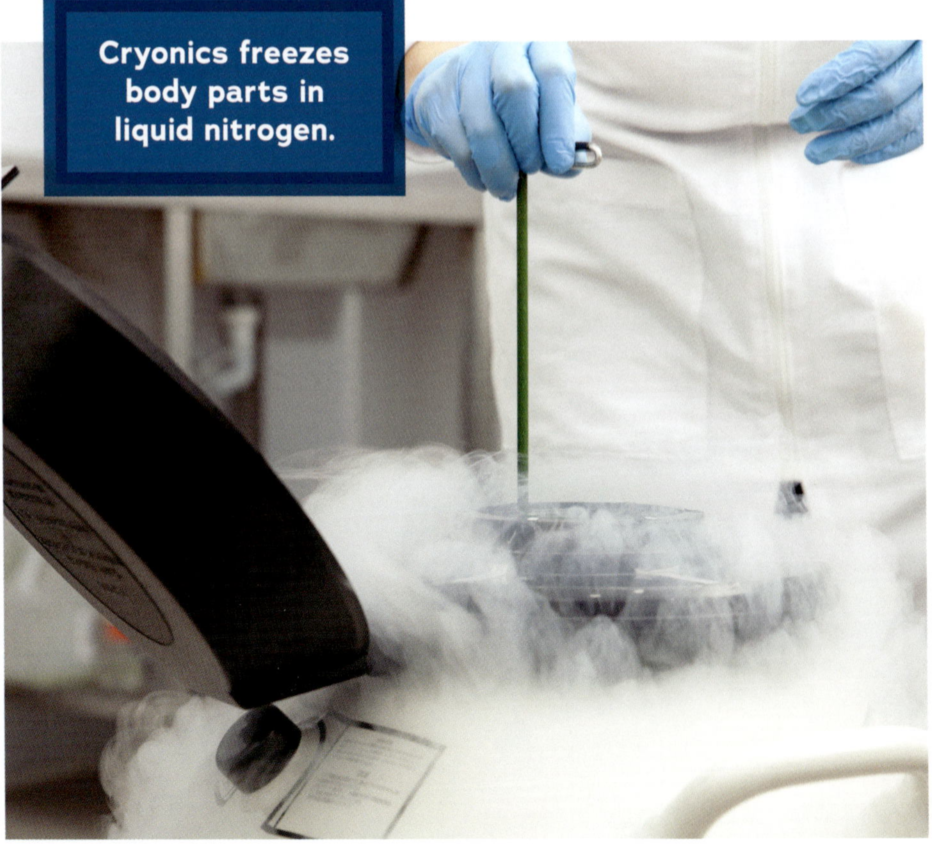

Cryonics freezes body parts in liquid nitrogen.

But What If We Did?

Creating the right technology is only the first step to humans living forever. We also have to consider how they would live. People would need to keep working to pay for food, clothes, and many other things. Could people afford to live forever? Would it be boring to live forever, or even for one thousand years? Would we run out of space or resources, such as water and food?

Glossary

3D printer: a printer that can create a physical object

antibiotic: a medicine that fights diseases caused by bacteria

artificial: made by humans and not made of natural materials

artificial intelligence: a technology that enables robots and other machines to learn and think like humans

biological: having to do with living things

gene: a unit inside body cells that control how new cells are made

immune system: system in the body that protects from diseases

implant: something placed in the body

prosthetic: an artificial body part, such as a leg

sanitation: cleaning processes, such as clean water and washing hands

Learn More

Britannica Kids: Aging
https://kids.britannica.com/kids/article/aging/390638

Kane, Patrick. *Human 2.0: A Celebration of Human Bionics*. Mayo Clinic Press Kids, 2025.

Kids News: Cryonics Expert Reveals When Frozen Humans May Be Brought Back to Life
https://www.kidsnews.com.au/science/cryonics-expert-reveals-when-frozen-humans-may-be-brought-back-to-life/news-story/c18a97f0ab0aec98c26cd8d0e9938c74

Nichols, Ainsley. *Explore Cryobiology*. Lerner Publications, 2024.

Schwartz, Heather E. *Medical Artificial Intelligence Breakthroughs*. Mayo Clinic Press Kids, 2024.

National Geographic Kids: Could Humans Live Forever?
https://kids.nationalgeographic.com/books/article/could-humans-live-forever#:~:text=No%20matter%20how%20advanced%20technology,to%20live%3A%20perhaps%20125%20years

Index

Photo Acknowledgments

Image credits: hurricanehank/Shutterstock, p. 5; Boryana Manzurova/Shutterstock, Ditty_about_summer/Shutterstock, p. 5; Pi-Lens/Shutterstock, p. 7; Artem.G/New York Times/Public Domain/Wikipedia, p. 8; incamerastock/Alamy, p. 9; maks ph/Shutterstock, p. 11; Tyler Olson/Shutterstock, p. 12; Jens Ottoson/Shutterstock, p, 13; Vichie81/Shutterstock, p. 14; Christoffer Hansen/Shutterstock, p. 15; ruek66/Shutterstock, p. 17; Associated Press/Alamy, p. 18; Karen Foley/Dreamstime, p. 19; Royal Geographic Society/Alamy, p. 20; SZakharov/Shutterstock, p. 21; Lua Carlos Martins/Shutterstock, p. 23; Dmitri Khramov/Dreamstime, p. 24; Timo Palo/Creative Commons/Wikipedia, p. 25; Pictorial Press Ltd/Alamy, p. 26; Anton_Antonov/Shutterstock, p. 27; Classic Image/Alamy, p. 28; Mozgova /Dreamstime, p. 29.

Cover: Aleksandr Ozerov/Shutterstock.